Leadership Works

Advanced Study Guide for *L.E.A.D.*

52 Leadership Lessons That
Last a Lifetime

Glen Aubrey

www.Lead52.com
www.CreativeTeamPublishing.com

Creative
Team
Publishing

Creative Team Publishing
San Diego

First Printing

ISBN: 978-0-9797358-3-7
PUBLISHED BY CREATIVE TEAM PUBLISHING
www.CreativeTeamPublishing.com
San Diego

Printed in the United States of America

Leadership Works

Advanced Study Guide for *L.E.A.D.*

52 Leadership Lessons That
Last a Lifetime

Glen Aubrey

www.Lead52.com
www.CreativeTeamPublishing.com

Dedication

Leadership Works is dedicated to leaders and teams that desire to learn, educate, act, and create destiny.

These teams are made up of committed people who are growing to understand the value of people and production.

They are convinced that relationships matter most and that functions are vital.

They are committed to achieving excellence in who they are and what they do.

They unreservedly agree that the decisions they make about each other's success compose the origins of superior provision no matter their fields of endeavor.

They know that leading teams well is hard work.

They embrace the call and challenge to contribute within relational and functional balance.

They know that building great leadership and maturing teams requires changes in their behaviors.

They are sure that investing in people yields great people and enhanced production.

They work hard, enjoy the journey, and celebrate their success.

Description

Congratulations on purchasing *Leadership Works*, an advanced study guide and learning companion to *L.E.A.D.—Learning, Education, Action, Destiny*.

The curriculum and the book comprise 52 leadership studies, principles in practical application, one lesson for each week of the year. *Leadership Works* and *L.E.A.D.* are available for purchase at **www.Lead52.com** or through the Creative Team Resources Group (CTRG) online store, **www.ctrg.com**.

Table of Contents

Opening

Let's define several key terms and a foundational principle used in *L.E.A.D.*—*Learning, Education, Action, Destiny*. At Creative Team Resources Group, Inc. (**CTRG, www.ctrg.com**) we use the words *relationship* and *function* consistently, as well as *Core Team*. Here are their meanings:

- *Relationship* is defined as the decision one makes about the success of another.
- *Function* is defined as the task that proves the validity of the decision.
- *Core Team* describes a group of growing individuals who work together based on these structural, relational, and functional foundations:

  C—Consistency in relationships and functions

  O—Obedience to core values

  R—Right relationships that endure

  E—Example, where the question is not if one has an example, but "What kind of example does he or she have?"

  T—Trust offered freely when a relationship begins and proven over time as a relationship extends

  E—Essentials of composite nature, comprising experience, education, and environment

  A—Accountability, "...repeatable proof over time that a person and his or her performance can be counted upon, that consistent results will accompany the process of endeavor." (From *Core Teams Work*, page 102, see below.)

  M—Methods, functions and contributions performed with excellence

The single and unalterable premise upon which we frame our teachings and practices is this: People are more important than production and relationship precedes and gives birth to function.

These truths and their definitions are essential to understanding the concepts and associated applications referenced throughout this study guide. They also resonate within three prior books:

- *Leadership Is— How to Build Your Legacy (***www.LeadershipIs.com***)*
- *Industrial Strength Solutions Build Successful Work Teams!* **(www.IndustrialStrengthSolutions.com***)*
- *Core Teams Work Their Principles and Practices (***www.CoreTeamsWork.com***)*

You are invited to refer to these books to enhance learning and encourage remembrance as you embrace what you read and study.

Embark on a journey of life and leadership discovery. Delve eagerly into learning, education, and action. When you do, you create a process of growth, a destiny for yourself and those who follow.

Take the lessons you observe on the page and make them the actions you purposefully engage. Positive results emerge over time in your life and the lives of those you impact.

Learning

Great teachers are dedicated students. Great leaders are committed followers. Instructors teach lessons they are convinced are true and worthy of application. They invest into the lives of those who look to them for information and example.

A quest for learning is insatiable in the heart of the eager student. People who want to mature express little contentment for the status quo of what they know. They want more.

How do you learn? When most groups we work with are asked this question, the usual replies reference learning from mistakes. Have you considered how often you learn from victories and successes as well? Both sources are important in a balanced learning process.

If there were an outline of effective learning techniques, what would it look like? Consider this one:

1. Teacher and student discover their interconnecting points, the common threads of interest and application that bring them together. They agree on basic principles, the values they both believe are immovable. Their agreements promote conceptual receptivity and practical use of what they learn.

2. Teacher and student develop cooperative relationships and functions. The teacher makes a great decision about the success of the student, taking time and supplying tools to help the student grasp, retain, and act on truth. The student makes a great decision about the teacher's success (as well as his or her own) when the student learns well, is grateful for the instruction, thanks the teacher, and diligently applies learning in his or her environments.

3. Teacher and student willfully consider varied perspectives as they pursue discovery of truth. Open communication and forthright discussion foster atmospheres of thoughtful inquiry and purposeful decision making.

4. Teacher and student consistently evaluate growth in their processes of learning and achievement. They chart courses for continual quests to learn more. They assure that information imparted and received is practiced in life.

Leadership Is— describes the Course of Attainment beginning on page 173. There are five states of the course: Dreams, Desires, Goals, Action, and Reality. Learning is about moving from dreams toward reality. Learners set goals, act on them, evaluate progress, correct errors, and celebrate successes. They design and improve methods of growth. They expand their knowledge and use wisdom in application. People who learn, mature.

Whether you are leading or following, educating or learning, you remain a diligent student of principle and practice when you earnestly seek information and use it to build up the members of your team. Learning individuals attract others of like passion. They compose a group of dedicated people on a core team. Regardless of title, tenure, position, or station, the one who learns educates others for mutual benefits. Processes of learning never cease for members of a core team who desire strong relationships and consistent functions.

Education

Leaders are eager to impart truth to receptive followers. Educators long to see the success of their instruction in changed behaviors of those they reach and teach.

Education is the act of imparting knowledge into receptive hearts and minds. Great teachers educate their students because they want to see them to grow.

Students and followers are served well when teachers and leaders present meaningful information. Learners are served best when wisdom accompanies that instruction. Wisdom is the understanding of how to use information well. Knowledge without wisdom does not profit anyone who possesses information but fails to apply it appropriately. The most effective instructors teach information and the methods to put it into life.

A great educator instills designs for duplication into the minds and motions of those who are taught. This leader, by expression and example, expects that his or her followers will one day become instructors themselves. So they model the behaviors they want their students to emulate. They plan their content and methods to best fit the needs and aspirations of the learners.

Education is readily available. There is simply no limit to the sources and courses on virtually any topic of interest. The key is to find or create the right teaching methods and tools that work most effectively for teacher and student, leader and follower.

An educator who cares more is one who relies less on dusty, worn out, and moldy instructional methods that may not resonate with a student. A teacher who views education holistically employs fresher and fuller means of imparting truth, *so that the experiences of education are as valuable as the information shared within them.*

Education should not be confined within edifices of brick and mortar. Indeed, classrooms may be completely unorthodox. Innovative minds formulate and encourage creative methods to educate eager learners.

Inspiration and encouragement well up from the heart of a teacher who truly wants the best for the ones who are learning. Think of educators who have inspired you and how they did it. What methods characterized their education styles?

A dedicated instructor considers multiple means of educating. He or she chooses techniques that assure receptivity and work for the greatest results.

Action

Changed and improved behaviors are abiding proofs of effective learning and education. Action and production are natural results of information instilled into ready minds, then distilled into patterns of living.

If action doesn't occur, communication and learning are not complete. Those who learn much and educate well expect to observe positive behavioral changes in teachers and students, leaders and followers.

Action, of course, is doing something, not just thinking about it. Ideas remain concepts until a person acts.

Behaviors are demonstrations of effective learning and education. What a person does shows just how much they've taken in and how much they'll give back again.

Put another way, action is function emerging from solid relationships. A decision to learn all one can and educate those who want to grow (relationship) is seen when an instructor helps others achieve their dreams and goals (function). This is success.

Destiny

Learning, education, and action create models of engagement. Together they provide proof tests of accountability and endurance. These proof tests are the elements of destiny.

Destiny constitutes a conclusion of a process, but it is also made up of the process itself. Think of destiny not only as a consequence but as the means of achieving desired ends.

Great leaders never stop learning. They never cease to educate eager followers. Their actions, based on what they receive and give, form frameworks of investment where benefits are shared from one generation to the next.

The journey is the destination, a part of creating a living legacy. Destiny combines learning, education, action, and results. Who you are and who you become constitute living proofs of positive outcomes, seen in the lives of those you touch.

Leadership Works
Advanced Study Guide

L.E.A.D.—Learning, Education, Action, Destiny and *Leadership Works* can be utilized in several effective ways.

- Individuals use the book and advanced study guide for personal learning and application.
- Core teams use the book and advanced study guide as a team building course, covering one lesson at each weekly staff meeting.
- Both publications are designed for use by leaders and their core teams. What leaders learn, they teach. What a team receives and acts upon creates destiny.

Each expanded study in *Leadership Works* is divided into three parts.

1. "Comments" are statements that encourage further consideration and action on the part of the participants. They are designed to build upon the lesson content in *L.E.A.D.*

2. "Questions" are interrogatories that help the core team think deeper, consider broad applications, and tackle difficult considerations. You and your team are encouraged to write out your answers to each question.

3. "Application" is probably the most important segment. *L.E.A.D.* focuses on learning, education, action, and destiny. In the study guide each participant is asked what he or she is learning, what they will teach and to whom, what actions (changes in their behaviors) they will decide, and what their expected results will be. Each team member is requested to write out their responses, and, where appropriate, indicate action timelines.

Learning, education, and action create destiny. These are the focus points of the studies.

Adapt the language and application to your setting and workplace language. Adopt the principles and practices into real life settings that compose your work world.

Take the book and this curriculum and make them your own. Chart your progress. Celebrate your success! Let's begin.

Lesson 1
Initiative

Comments:

1. Great leaders are disciplined followers. Great teachers are dedicated students.

2. Every follower becomes a leader when that follower takes initiative, regardless of title, tenure, position, or place.

3. When initiative becomes a way of thinking and acting, a culture of problem maintenance, tolerance, and complaining is replaced with a new environment of solution thinking and acting.

Questions:

1. What initiatives have you taken that have demonstrated your leadership?

2. How important is your initiative to the members of your core team?

3. What initiatives have you seen a leader take that you would like to emulate?

4. What initiatives would you consider taking to promote solution thinking and acting in your workplace?

Application:

Lessons I am learning:

Truths I will teach:

Actions I will take:

Results I will expect:

Lesson 2
Values

Comments:

1. Values are attributes of character, good or bad. Name three positive values and three negative ones.

2. Values are at the core of every action. List three positive and three negative actions and identify their associated values.

3. Deciding, defining, and ratifying desired values are essential exercises for an organization that wants to understand positive motives behind best methods.

Questions:

1. What values do the job functions of your core team demonstrate?

2. Which dysfunctional actions related to job functions reveal violations of your team's values?

3. If actions of team members do not align with core team values, what questions would cause an errant member to consider correcting negative contributions, transforming these into positive ones?

Application:

Lessons I am learning:

Truths I will teach:

Actions I will take:

Results I will expect:

Lesson 3
Vision, Mission, and Message

Comments:

1. The Preamble of the United States Constitution is one of the finest vision statements ever composed. Look it up and write it out.

2. Examine and define the values articulated within it.

3. The mission of an organization is demonstrated in its actions.

4. *Consistency* of mission is shown where the activities of the individual support those of the team and those of the team support the mission of the organization.

5. Message can be a motto, hallmark, primary lesson, central core truth, or any of these in combination.

6. Message is focused on a specific target.

7. Message is what people recall when they think of your core team or company.

Questions:

1. How tied are your team's actions to the overall vision of the organization?

2. What alterations in attitudes and actions would occur if vision was fully understood and embraced by the team?

3. To what degree is vision an integral part of recurring team discussions?

4. How willing is your team to discard actions or programs that do not support the vision of the organization?

5. What specific actions in the last month has the team accomplished that have demonstrated confidence in the mission of the organization?

6. In the same time frame, what specific actions from the team have not contributed to fulfilling the organization's mission?

7. Why is it important to cease non-supportive actions?

8. What are three mottos or messages that instantly cause you to recall a particular company?

9. On a scale of 1 to 10, scoring 10 as the highest, how effective is your team or organization's message in helping others recognize your team or company?

Application:

Lessons I am learning:

Truths I will teach:

Actions I will take:

Results I will expect:

Lesson 4
A Value System

Comments:

1. A value system is a code of conduct born of principles. Actions are principles in application.

2. A value system encourages right and consistent behaviors based on lasting truths on which the team agrees and to which they adhere.

3. When thinking aligns to a value system, consistent and accountable behavior becomes possible to achieve. Thinking and acting on the basis of a value system require reminders of the system's standards and evaluations of a person's conduct.

Questions:

1. What is the value system of your team?

2. What is your value system?

3. What are the specific intersecting points of your value system and the value system of the team?

4. What tools serve as reminders of your team's code of conduct?

Application:

Lessons I am learning:

Truths I will teach:

Actions I will take:

Results I will expect:

A Value System

Twelve Laws of Understanding

1. Realize I am responsible for my own choices, not others'; that changing someone else's behavior is not my responsibility; rather, I need to change me.
2. Seek to understand how the other person thinks and communicates; use his or her language.
3. Model what I want.
4. Set realistic limits on what is acceptable behavior.
5. Impose these limits on myself, first.
6. Desire the best, but prepare for difficulty; seek creative, peaceful solutions.
7. Seek and pray for wisdom.
8. Remember, at the right times.
9. Encourage always.
10. Think first, listen most, and speak seldom.
11. Realize growth involves change, change can mean pain, and patience on the journey is a virtue.
12. Love. Establish meaningful relationships.

Lesson 5
Leaders Are Followers First

Comments:

1. Since leaders teach followers how to follow before they teach them how to lead, effective leaders look for ways to show what positive and contribution-focused following looks like.

2. The attributes of a great leader should be seen in the follower.

3. Exemplary followers become leaders to others who observe their behaviors.

4. Attentive following is a state where mentoring can occur and legacy can be built.

Questions:

1. What aspects of learning how to follow present the most formidable challenges to the student of leadership?

2. What responsibility does a follower have, if any, to confront a leader who is not following well?

3. How should a confrontation discussion take place, in what atmosphere, with whom, and with what attitudes and actions in evidence?

4. Since following well is the mark of maturing leadership, how often should instruction take place on its methods and benefits?

Application:
Lessons I am learning:

Truths I will teach:

Actions I will take:

Results I will expect:

Lesson 6
Praise

Comments:

1. List the benefits of praise that is freely given.

2. Describe the characteristics of a work environment where praise is not willingly and willfully given or received.

3. Discover the impediments to receiving praise.

4. Discuss the barriers that make giving praise awkward.

5. Handle hindrances to giving and receiving praise with encouragement and creative thinking. List specific actions that should be taken to build up positive atmospheres of praise.

Questions:

1. Why is the notion false that it is not appropriate to affirm leadership and praise them for their value as persons and the worth of their contributions?

2. How often are praise and affirmation expressed on your team?

3. What are preferred ways of receiving and giving praise on your core team? How do you know?

4. What creative methods would stimulate engaging in affirmation? How willing is the team to list them and employ them on a recurring basis?

Application:

Lessons I am learning:

Truths I will teach:

Actions I will take:

Results I will expect:

Lesson 7
Decisions

Comments:

1. The status of your business exists as a result of prior decisions. Name the most impactful ones over the last two years, whether negative or positive, that contributed to your team's current condition.

2. The decisions you make today determine your audience and your effectiveness tomorrow.

3. The procedures you and your core team employ in decision making indicate what you value least and most.

4. Decisions are communicated in words and actions, attitudes and character.

Questions:

1. What processes should the leader and team use to weigh the worth of a decision before it is made?

2. How important is considering who and what will be affected by major decisions?

3. What processes should a leader or team employ to help decision making be productive?

4. How important is weighing decisions against values, vision, mission, and message?

5. What are preferred methods of communicating the decisions made by you and your teams?

Application:

Lessons I am learning:

Truths I will teach:

Actions I will take:

Results I will expect:

Lesson 8
Business Growth

Comments:

1. Reliable business growth is not accidental, nor is it based on luck. It is the result of purposed planning and plain hard work.

2. Businesses grow through building production and profit, as well as making good decisions about the people who make the processes work.

3. An organization considers its past and present, people and production, and potential for expansion. These factors determine the choices an entity makes as it moves into its future.

4. Establishing a business growth environment is not optional for leaders and teams who want to expand their customer service effectiveness, raise profits, and build long term positive effects.

5. Name specific effectiveness proofs that your team enjoys now as a result of solid business growth decisions in the past.

Questions:

1. What business growth decisions, made before the current leadership was installed, contributed to greatness and success? Who made these decisions, and in what circumstances?

2. What business growth decisions in your organization's history contributed to stalemates, status quo, discouragement, or shortchanged results?

3. How much should current leadership rely and build upon business growth decisions of the past?

4. How should a core team's code of achievement be incorporated into growing its business?

5. What are detailed examples of service to the staff that have developed into increased services to customers within the last 60 days?

6. What makes up a healthy business growth environment?

7. What kind of a business growth environment do you have? What would make it superior?

Application:

Lessons I am learning:

Truths I will teach:

Actions I will take:

Results I will expect:

Lesson 9
Agreement

Comments:

1. The DNA of a team is comprised of its values, vision, mission, and message, its Code of Achievement. Values are the principles upon which a team agrees and to which it adheres. Vision is the reason an organization exists. Mission is what the organization does. Message is what the organization learns and teaches.

2. A core team must first go through the exercise of identifying, defining, and ratifying its values. These constitute the foundations on which to build vision, mission, and message.

3. To identify values it is often helpful to utilize existing models of these statements. (Please see **www.ctrg.com** for the Creative Team Resources Group, Inc. Values, Vision, Mission, and Message statements.)

4. Once essential core values have been identified, they must be defined. In this process, use of tools like a dictionary, thesaurus, and existing statements from other organizations is encouraged. Definitions must include words and phrases that represent the character, constitution, language, and communication styles of the group.

5. Once identified and defined, ratification of your team's values is next. Ratifying the values firmly establishes their importance and strategic worth. These agreed values form the constitution of your organization. While amendments to this constitution can be made, a change process should not be quick and

easy. Indeed, procedures used to remove, add, redefine, or rework any value must include identification, definition, and thorough deliberation.

6. Once the values agreement process is completed, the team moves to articulate and define its vision, mission, and message. This sequence is important. The process of establishing these vital elements works best when this order is followed.

7. Once completed the team understands better who they are (values), their reason for existence (vision), their actions of provision (mission), and the truths they learn and educate (message).

Questions:

1. When will your team engage in the process of identifying, defining, and ratifying its values, if this important step has not yet been taken?

2. Were you to describe the process of values identification, definition, and ratification, what actions have you seen or do you want to see?

3. Why is it essential that values agreement precedes efforts to compose and agree on vision, mission, and message?

4. Why are core values related to the essence of a team?

5. Why is vision related to what a person or team believes they are called to do?

6. How is mission related to what a person or team wants?

7. In what ways is message related to the target the team will impact?

Application:

Lessons I am learning:

Truths I will teach:

Actions I will take:

Results I will expect:

Lesson 10
Character Is Revealed When Conflict Comes

Comments:

1. Name the negative attitudes often displayed in dealing with conflict.

2. Describe actions that validate agreed values in the midst of difficulty.

3. Inquire which specific behaviors must be changed to realign with the values the team holds, especially in conflict.

4. Ask each person to write down behaviors that they will commit to change in dealing with difficult issues.

5. Ask the team members to articulate the preferred behaviors they desire to demonstrate when difficulties arise, then evaluate their success or failure when the storm passes.

Questions:

1. What behaviors are seen most readily when confronting conflict negatively?

2. What exemplary behaviors are shown when dealing with conflict from a positive and solution-focused mind set?

3. What are examples of conflict engagement and resolution in which the core team has clearly demonstrated preferred behaviors?

4. What celebrations has the team enjoyed from their winning efforts?

Application:

Lessons I am learning:

Truths I will teach:

Actions I will take:

Results I will expect:

Lesson 11
Conflict Resolution

Comments:

1. Dealing with conflict reveals core behaviors because images and facades are stripped away.

2. Define the positive character traits of dignity, self-respect, and courtesy.

3. Assure that agreement exists on these definitions.

4. Define the negative character traits of ego driven pride, disrespect, and dishonor.

5. Assure that agreement exists on these definitions.

6. Describe turf protection and covering up wrong doing by illustrating an example from current national or local news.

7. Discuss and agree on methods that discourage protecting fiefdoms, that encourage breaking down silos and abolishing selfish isolationism.

Questions:

1. In the middle of severe difficulty what would cause a team to exhibit respectful behavior?

2. How should a group deal with negative behaviors demonstrated by team members who handle conflict inappropriately?

3. What are clear indications that courtesy is a primary motivator when team members handle conflict well?

4. Were you to describe the observable actions that showcase courtesy, what are they?

Application:

Lessons I am learning:

Truths I will teach:

Actions I will take:

Results I will expect:

Lesson 12
Frameworks

Comments:

1. The term *ownership* describes a state of solution provision where the person with the problem designs the solution and, upon acceptance of that solution, participates willingly to achieve positive results.

2. Consider what it would look like if a leader owned the success of the follower.

3. Describe a healthy condition where a leader creates a framework in which a follower can succeed. Explain what the follower's responsibilities are within this arrangement.

4. Assure agreement exists on definitions and practical applications of these words: *opportunity*, a *win*, *instruction*, and *guidance*.

Questions:

1. What is an example of unhealthy ownership?

2. How do manipulation and micromanaging demonstrate disease on a team?

3. What is a current example of a leader who constructed a framework in which a follower achieved success?

4. How should a follower and leader cooperate to gain success?

5. What are the hallmarks of health in a leader-follower relationship?

Application:

Lessons I am learning:

Truths I will teach:

Actions I will take:

Results I will expect:

Lesson 13
Investment

Comments:

1. A *willing* follower is one who agrees with the leader on the tenets of an investment.

2. The quality of a relationship determines how willing a follower is to receive a leader's investment.

3. A willing follower demonstrates strong decisions about the success of the leader.

4. A leader who tries to motivate an unwilling follower is wasting resources.

5. A *working* follower is one who exercises faithfulness as an investment process begins and proceeds.

6. A working follower demonstrates a solid work ethic.

7. A working follower showcases commitment to functioning well.

8. A leader who tolerates or excuses poor functioning from a follower is not investing.

Questions:

1. What are attributes of willingness that are easy to identify?

2. What are characteristics of contributory function that are easily seen?

3. What are responsibilities of the follower who is given an opportunity for investment?

4. What are the tell tale signs of a healthy investment?

5. What are the obvious signs that an investment is not working?

6. What should the leader do if a follower claims willingness but does not work toward achieving desired results?

7. How should a leader deal with a lack of balance in willingness or work ethic from a follower?

Application:

Lessons I am learning:

Truths I will teach:

Actions I will take:

Results I will expect:

Lesson 14
Interaction

Comments:

1. Positive interaction between a leader and members of the core team doesn't just happen. It is planned.

2. Name several examples of positive interaction that you have witnessed and would like to see duplicated on your team.

3. Planning great interaction does not prevent chance encounters; rather, it helps prepare for them.

4. An accountable leader builds foundations for positive interactions.

5. Positive interaction on a team illustrates agreement to principles.

Questions:

1. What are the values of your team that are demonstrated in member's positive interactions with one another?

2. What values are violated when negative interactions occur?

3. What are the differences between "talking the walk" and "walking the talk" in creating an environment of positive interaction?

4. Why are negative interactions like micromanaging and intimidation discouraged or eliminated when interactions are planned and agreed upon?

Application:

Lessons I am learning:

Truths I will teach:

Actions I will take:

Results I will expect:

Lesson 15
Relationship and Function

Comments:

1. The term *relationship* denotes either positive or negative decisions about another person's success.

2. Relationships are classified as contributory when positive and moral values uphold them, and they are proven in activity.

3. Because relationship and function cannot be separated, the choice for a leader or team member is whether to concentrate on improving relationships or functions first.

4. Longer lasting success comes when causes, not just symptoms, are addressed.

5. A cause is stimulated by desire; a symptom is the evidence of what the desire is or was.

6. Core teams who want great provision make better decisions about people's success. They know that contributory functions will follow and verify the strength of the decisions.

7. Name several functions of the people on your team that clearly demonstrate solid and contributory decisions about someone else's success.

Questions:

1. How can the quality of a relationship be measured apart from function?

2. What, if any, are the tasks of the members of your team that are not directly related to decisions about another's success or failure?

3. Because a team understands that functions and relationships are never separated, what does observing or participating in negative activities say about the relational decisions that have been made?

4. Why should strong relationships consistently produce contributory functions?

5. What is the benefit of investing in positive relational decisions as a means to correct dysfunction?

Application:

Lessons I am learning:

Truths I will teach:

Actions I will take:

Results I will expect:

Lesson 16
The Storehouse of Giving

Comments:

1. Describe the standards of service given to your organization's staff. Discuss what core values they illustrate.

2. Explain your organization's customer servicing standards and compare these to the standards of service given to the staff. Note where similarities and discrepancies exist.

3. Your physical facilities often mirror the degree of dedication to internal and external customer service. Note differences, if any, between staff work areas and customer reception or service areas, including restrooms and lounges.

4. Characterize conditions of internal staff areas and what they say about creating a welcoming and productive environment for the people who work in your company.

5. The commitment the staff employs in external customer service is a reflection of the commitment of internal service given to the staff.

Questions:

1. How often are internal customer servicing standards discussed at the staff level and what are the core team's conclusions?

2. What reasonable differences should exist between the quality of service external customers receive and what is offered to the staff who serve the customers?

3. What are the standards of external customer service that continue to challenge the team?

4. Which of the above items share links to challenges in meeting internal customer needs?

5. How important is the process of setting a customer servicing standard to the staff before expecting the staff to meet a customer servicing standard for a customer?

6. What specific actions would your team show to each other if they knew external customers would receive the same treatment?

7. How important are evaluations of internal and external customer service, how often should they be conducted, and by what methods?

Application:

    Lessons I am learning:

    Truths I will teach:

    Actions I will take:

    Results I will expect:

Lesson 17
Celebrations

Comments:

1. Describe the processes your organization undertakes in designing and executing a major business expansion initiative.

2. Articulate the processes your organization undertakes in designing and executing celebrations for its teams.

3. Discuss the differences and similarities of the processes.

4. Recall the elements of one of your company or team's most successful celebrations. Relate the effects this celebration had on members of the core team.

Questions:

1. What are the reasons for affirming people as people and recognizing and appreciating their contributions?

2. To what degree should affirmation of the people on your team be related only to contributions?

3. How should a team celebrate a member whose contributions fall short of desired excellence, or should they?

Application:

Lessons I am learning:

Truths I will teach:

Actions I will take:

Results I will expect:

Lesson 18

Seven-Step Process of Solution Provision—
Dealing With Incidents and Issues

Comments:

1. Describe two current challenging incidents in your organization.

2. Note the issue(s) each incident illustrates.

3. Discovering facts, uncovering causes, and articulating desires are not optional in a successful solution provision process. Ask your team which of the parts of this process represent the most difficulty and which are the easiest to accomplish, and why.

4. If closure is important to a team, ownership of tasks and faithful reporting cannot be separated.

5. Performance without excellence is substandard. Performance with excellence sets new standards.

6. Degrees of excellence of performance show how sincere a team is to improve.

7. Evaluation can be conducted in negative or positive atmospheres. Ask the team to list attributes of both, which they prefer, and why.

Questions:

1. Does the team dwell more in solving incidents or issues?

2. When issues are discovered, how often are they weighed against agreed values, vision, mission, and message?

3. Which of the seven steps are the most difficult ones for your team to accomplish and why?

4. If engaging in problem solving communication is a challenge for the team, what are the causes of this dysfunction?

5. Why are difficulties in problem resolution related to violations of agreed values, unclear vision, unknown and disjointed execution of mission, or an absence of message?

6. What are a leader's and follower's responsibilities in applying the Seven-Step Process of Solution Provision?

7. What issues have you and your team seen positively resolved as a result of applying the process fully?

Application:

Lessons I am learning:

Truths I will teach:

Actions I will take:

Results I will expect:

Lesson 19
A Core Team Leader's Responsibilities

Comments:

1. If you are the leader, describe the leadership qualities you desire your followers to emulate.

2. Authority and accountability are illustrations of relationship and function. Discuss why this is true.

3. A stop-by leader makes an impression on followers, positive or negative.

4. Describe the benefits a leader and follower enjoy when a leader who cares visits a follower's workplace.

5. Designing goals cooperatively is a sure sign of leader-follower health. Relate how cooperation is observed in behaviors of both leader and follower.

6. Charting progress is part of evaluation and is not optional if a team wants to improve.

7. Celebrations teach leaders and followers where their values lie.

Questions:

1. Why should job descriptions include relational as well as functional requirements for leaders and followers?

2. What are ways that a visit from a leader can be uncomfortable and unnecessary?

3. What are the benefits of a positive visit of a leader into a follower's work area?

4. What methods of designing and implementing goals does your team utilize?

5. What methods of charting progress and evaluating success or failure does your team employ and how successful are they?

6. What values do your celebrations portray?

7. What are areas of leadership that, if improved, would stimulate more positive responses from followers?

Application:

Lessons I am learning:

Truths I will teach:

Actions I will take:

Results I will expect:

Lesson 20
Close the Loops

Comments:

1. Closing communication loops shows dedication to another's success. Closure provides proof of a strong relationship between an assignor of a task and the one who fulfills it.

2. When a leader has to chase down a follower to get information, the follower is not making a decision to support the leader's success. It may be that the leader has never taught the follower how to responsibly close the loops.

3. Teaching processes of closing the loops is the responsibility of the leader. These processes include:
   a. Defining which projects require communication loop closure.
   b. Instructing which communication methods to use: email, written hard copy, phone, fax, in person, or combinations of these.
   c. Constructing communication lines for reporting, identifying who should give and receive reports.
   d. Establishing timelines of reporting.
   e. Setting evaluation systems in place.

4. Leaders who instruct followers how to close loops assure that the examples they provide to the followers are those they want to receive.

Questions:

1. Why is communication better served when closing the loops is accomplished?

2. What are the effects when closure does not occur?

3. What are examples of tasks that do not require closing the loops?

4. How often and in what forums should instruction occur on methods of closure?

Application:

Lessons I am learning:

Truths I will teach:

Actions I will take:

Results I will expect:

Lesson 21
Thankfulness

Comments:

1. Name specific examples of thankfulness freely expressed in your workplace and what forms these expressions took.

2. One can be thankful for a person, a deed, or both.

3. Thanksgiving is the art of giving and receiving.

4. Thankfulness should never be assumed; rather, it should be taught, rehearsed, and practiced diligently.

Questions:

1. What are ways of determining how to thank a person for who they are and what they do?

2. How important is it to thank the person as well as recognize the deed?

3. What are the barriers to giving and receiving thanksgiving?

4. What are preferred methods to overcome and erase these barriers?

5. Why is thankfulness a mark of maturity on a team?

Application:

Lessons I am learning:

Truths I will teach:

Actions I will take:

Results I will expect:

Lesson 22
Success Through Mentoring

Comments:

1. Mentoring is life upon life investment and requires values agreement from the mentor and the person who is mentored.

2. A mentoring relationship is time sensitive—it has a defined start date and an established end date.

3. A mentoring relationship outlines specific goals of investment. These include learning, education, and the application of principles into real life.

4. Mentoring is successful when the works from the one who is mentored become greater than those of the one who is mentoring.

5. Mentoring requires strong relationships and exemplary functions. It will not settle for mediocrity in either.

6. A mentoring process is difficult and costly but, with the right persons engaged for the right reasons, it is worth its required costs.

7. A mentoring relationship requires absolute agreement on the essentials of its construction and implementation. A leader and follower should define in writing:
    a. Values shared by leader and follower
    b. Goals of the engagement

      c. Timeline

      d. Reporting mechanisms

      e. Definitions of success

      f. Evaluation procedures

      g. Celebrations

Questions:

1. Understanding the role and goal of mentoring, how many people realistically should one person mentor at one time?

2. When should a leader consider a mentoring engagement?

3. How should a follower who wants to mature approach a leader to request mentoring?

4. If you were to outline a mentoring plan, whether you were the mentor or receiver, what would this plan consist of and how would it work?

5. Who is someone from whom you would like to receive mentoring?

6. What would the goals of a mentoring relationship be for you in a mentoring engagement?

7. If you are the mentor, who are you mentoring now and what are your reasonable expectations of results?

Application:

Lessons I am learning:

Truths I will teach:

Actions I will take:

Results I will expect:

Lesson 23
Nurture and Support

Comments:

1. Identify nurturing environments you have been part of and the results you have experienced.

2. A successful nurturing process can be difficult because it involves respectful confrontation, invasion with permission, into the life and action of someone else for their benefit.

3. When nurturing is accomplished within a strong relationship, defense posturing should occur seldom, if at all.

4. When nurture is imposed in the absence of a relationship defense posturing is common.

5. Support is offered in good and bad times.

6. Support consists of mutual understanding, encouragement, and interdependent actions that demonstrate the strength of the relationship.

7. Support usually feels good and is often shared mutually.

8. Support builds credibility, is an evidence of positive character, and fosters open and uplifting communication.

Questions:

1. When a nurturing process is contemplated, how should a leader approach a follower to begin?

2. What environments are best in which to nurture?

3. What atmospheres would impede or prevent successful nurturing?

4. What are examples of support on your team?

5. If you are one who recently received support, what were your reactions when the help was offered?

6. Because nurture confronts wrongs and encourages healing, and support tells someone they are cared for, how should a leader communicate his or her intentions when these processes are needed?

7. What places do nurturing and supporting activities have on your team?

Application:

Lessons I am learning:

Truths I will teach:

Actions I will take:

Results I will expect:

Lesson 24

Engaged Leadership—The Process of Connecting

Comments:

1. Establishing connection on a team requires initiative from the leader.

2. A follower can take the initiative to connect, too.

3. Connection obliterates silos and stovepipes. Describe why this is true and what the results are of removing silos and stovepipes.

4. The Four Questions can be used to foster open communication and encourage connection. Describe how and why these will work in your environment.

5. Positive connection establishes and reinforces mutual growth and dignity.

6. When connection is working well, relationships are strengthened and functions improve.

7. Describe positive workplace connections within your core team.

Questions:

1. Why could imposed connecting develop negative consequences?

2. What are the differences between connecting for mutual benefits and connecting to intimidate or micromanage?

3. Because motives and means of connecting illustrate intent, how should a leader promote positive connection in the workplace?

4. How often should your team use the Four Questions to open up lines of communication and engagement?

5. What are the results of positive connection and mentoring?

Application:

Lessons I am learning:

Truths I will teach:

Actions I will take:

Results I will expect:

Lesson 25
Creating Workplace Positives

Comments:

1. Big things often come in small packages. Relate this common truth to creating workplace positives.

2. Name seemingly small behaviors that, when demonstrated, illustrate uplifting workplace attitudes.

3. Identify other small behaviors that, when observed, illustrate negative workplace relationships.

4. List 10 workplace positives that are common to your team and its working environment.

5. "Give what you want returned to you." Describe why this technique is effective.

Questions:

1. If practicing workplace positives seems like the obvious thing to do, why can doing them be difficult?

2. What are inhibitors to contributing small, positive behaviors that touch others daily?

3. What kind of commitments to changing behavior would a core team have to establish to encourage workplace positives?

4. What roles, if any, does personality play in exercising workplace positives?

5. To what degree should personality even be a factor?

6. How does a team honor its members when positive behaviors are practiced?

7. If positive behaviors are decisions about another's success, what does not engaging in them demonstrate?

Application:

Lessons I am learning:

Truths I will teach:

Actions I will take:

Results I will expect:

Lesson 26

Recognizing and Pursuing Personal Opportunity

Comments:

1. Opportunities outnumber viable options.

2. Opportunities are related to capability.

3. Viable options can be revealed through call.

4. Initiative is required in recognition and pursuit of opportunity.

5. More initiative is required in fulfilling call.

6. Fulfilling potential rests on desire.

7. Opportunities and options remain as hopes and dreams unless a person sets specific and time sensitive goals, and acts on them.

8. Interviewing successful people in your field of interest is a good way to understand strengths, weaknesses, opportunities, and threats of any desired engagement.

9. Name several of your opportunities.

10. Name the activities that you believe you are called to do, that you are passionate about.

Questions:

1. What creates motivation in a person to move beyond what they know into realms they should go?

2. Who are the instrumental players who have helped you venture beyond your status quo?

3. When potential is present in a follower, but not activated, what is the responsibility, if any, of the leader who sees this?

4. What are the roles of followers who earnestly desire growth and maturity?

5. How important is receiving counsel from trusted advisors in moving from capability to call?

6. Because capability and call often reside together, what is the learner's responsibility regarding fulfilling tasks, whether related to capability, call, or both?

7. How could completing the goals of opportunity and achieving the objectives of a calling comprise the same set of actions?

Application:

Lessons I am learning:

Truths I will teach:

Actions I will take:

Results I will expect:

Lesson 27
Integrity

Comments:

1. A working definition of *integrity* is "Words and deeds that match." Think of other definitions that clearly define what your team means by integrity.

2. Think of examples where integrity was violated because ends were more important than means.

3. Relate integrity to truth telling regarding:
    a. Progress reports
    b. Job completion
    c. Communication loop closure
    d. Responsible work ethic
    e. Time management
    f. Budgeting and financial reporting

4. Describe how integrity applied on the job does not tolerate behaviors known to be dishonest or untrustworthy.

Questions:

1. In what working environments is integrity most often set aside, if it is?

2. How is integrity restored if it is discovered to be compromised?

3. How does communicating realistic expectations of task fulfillment illustrate integrity?

4. What is the responsibility, if any, of a follower who sees his or her leader not exercising integrity?

5. What are the negative consequences of compromised integrity?

Application:

Lessons I am learning:

Truths I will teach:

Actions I will take:

Results I will expect:

Lesson 28

Great People and Great Production

Comments:

1. It is possible to achieve great production and not build people in the process. Describe the short term and long term effects of this imbalance.

2. Building people and production at the same time costs more and is worth much as the processes unfold.

3. If an organization has great people who are not producing well, this is a mark of relational and functional disconnect.

4. If an organization utilizes processes that consume their people, this also represents relational and functional disconnect.

5. Identify the worthy sacrifices that may be required to build people and production simultaneously.

6. Quantify the results from building both people and production that can be measured in dollars and cents.

7. Evaluate how your organization leans: more to building production or more to building people.

8. Describe how balancing people and production would benefit your team.

Questions:

1. When people are viewed as valuable for only what they produce, what are the tell tale signs of this perspective that can be seen in the actions of leaders and followers?

2. When people are treated as valued persons, what should be the realistic expectations of improved functional output?

3. When "people are more important than production" is used as an excuse for inactivity, how should this misapplication be addressed?

4. Because business production includes people and processes, relationships and functions, what is the leader's role in learning the balance, teaching it, and applying it with the team?

Application:
Lessons I am learning:

Truths I will teach:

Actions I will take:

Results I will expect:

Lesson 29
Rewarding Achievement

Comments:

1. Identify one project where, upon completion, no one was thanked, where contributors instead were ignored as another job action was started.

2. Name effective and meaningful ways that your team honors success.

3. Name the honorees at your last celebration and what they were honored for.

4. Describe tangible rewards that could accompany celebrations.

5. Describe intangible rewards that could accompany celebrations.

6. How an organization celebrates its people is a good indicator of how much the people are valued.

7. Respect and recognition of fulfilled goals and faithful service are seen in rewards, small and large.

Questions:

1. Where rewards are not given and achievements forgotten or ignored, what is the responsibility, if any, of the team leader or followers to address this issue?

2. How should budget cuts effect a continuing commitment to honor people and their accomplishments?

3. What are preferred means of recognizing achievement? Consider these options and provide your own:
    a. Verbal praise in front of peers
    b. Written citations
    c. Tangible gifts of value
    d. Intangible expressions of affirmation
    e. Hand written notes
    f. Phone calls
    g. Email

4. What are the impediments to rewarding achievement?

5. What are the benefits of engaging in spontaneous reward activities?

6. How does rewarding the person and the work accent relationship and function?

7. How should a leader match rewards with persons and their contributions?

Application:

Lessons I am learning:

Truths I will teach:

Actions I will take:

Results I will expect:

Lesson 30
Interdependence

Comments:

1. Dependence, independence, and interdependence are not isolated environments; rather, leaders and followers may operate in more than one at the same time.

2. Interdependence is a strong relationship between teacher and student, leader and follower, a place where greater education and wisdom are imparted.

3. Mentoring occurs and lasting legacy is built in the state of interdependence.

4. Interdependence produces agreed results in a predetermined timeline.

5. Name a leader who invested in you and with whom you enjoyed a state of interdependence.

6. Categorize your leader-follower relationships now in terms of dependence, independence, or interdependence.

7. If you are the leader, identify which of your followers you'd like to move into a relationship of interdependence.

8. If you are the follower, identify how much you want to move into more development with your leader.

Questions:

1. Why do the actions of interdependence require more time and resources?

2. What percentage of time should a leader set aside to help a follower mature within a relationship of interdependence?

3. Why should greater works be expected when a relationship of interdependence is completed?

4. Since relationships of interdependence have specific start and end dates, agreed goals, and measurable results, how should keeping track of achievements, correcting errors, and celebrating achievements be accomplished?

Application:

Lessons I am learning:

Truths I will teach:

Actions I will take:

Results I will expect:

Lesson 31
The Essence of Great Leadership

Comments:

1. Identify what ordinary leadership is.

2. Discuss the differences between great leadership that builds people and production and lesser leadership that focuses on function only.

3. Describe the specific actions of a great leader who cares about his or her followers.

4. If you are the leader, tell your followers how much you value them.

5. If you are the follower, declare how you would like to be valued for who you are and what you do.

Questions:

1. How should great leadership encourage followers to reach beyond comfort, complacency, and mediocrity?

2. How does your team know that "People are more important than production" is more than a phrase?

3. What models of behavior do lesser leaders project?

4. How much of great leadership is teaching followers to grow through example versus words alone?

5. What are a follower's responsibilities in helping a leader lead better?

Application:

Lessons I am learning:

Truths I will teach:

Actions I will take:

Results I will expect:

Lesson 32
Change Is Challenging

Comments:

1. Planning for the future means rehearsing for change.

2. Recall changes your team has endured and the benefits derived from the processes.

3. Ideas for change originate from many sources. Among them are altered circumstances, renewed commitment to ideals, and new personnel.

4. Describe the challenge that comes when change is imposed on a group.

5. Describe the opportunities for growth that occur when change is created by the group.

6. Positive change may not feel good.

7. Describe how a core team anchored on values, vision, mission, and message should approach needful, although uncomfortable, change.

Questions:

1. What attitudes toward change indicate a team member's willful agreement to engage in it? What attitudes demonstrate resistance?

2. When changes produce less than satisfactory results, how should a team handle discouragement, disappointment, frustration, and fault-finding?

3. If a team is not secure in their values, vision, mission, and message, what reactions can be expected when change is imminent?

4. In light of changes that are sure to come, what is the leader's role in helping his or her core team be prepared?

Application:

Lessons I am learning:

Truths I will teach:

Actions I will take:

Results I will expect:

Lesson 33
A Fresh Perspective

Comments:

1. Identify decisions currently affecting your team that should have been contemplated from a greater assimilation and evaluation of facts historically.

2. Leadership that is secure welcomes new viewpoints from productive team members.

3. One of the leader's responsibilities is to evaluate decisions against agreed values, vision, mission, and message.

4. A strong leader requests input from followers who have consistently provided best deliverables.

5. Name great leaders who have made decisions that produced positive effects.

6. Describe the current decision making phases your team employs when it considers a new course of action.

7. Fresh opportunities are best seized, weighed, decided, and acted upon when core team relationships are strong.

Questions:

1. What are barriers to considering alternate or diverse opinions?

2. Defensiveness makes its presence known in overt and covert ways. What are examples of both?

3. What attitudes or actions of your group would you like to improve in your decision making processes?

4. What attitudes and actions of your group demonstrate strong relationships and superior functions even when opinions vary and disagreements exist?

5. How should a leader encourage presentation, reception, and consideration of diverse ideas?

6. What is the responsibility of the core team once a decision is made?

7. When varying perspectives are discussed, what are the signs that a leader is insecure or easily threatened?

Application:

Lessons I am learning:

Truths I will teach:

Actions I will take:

Results I will expect:

Lesson 34
Reflections

Comments:

1. A company's external image often reflects the internal relationships between its leaders and followers.

2. A team's positive relationships are the foundations for strong internal and external functions.

3. Assess the quality of customer servicing the team believes it provides to your customers. Compare these results with what your customers say they receive. Note differences and similarities. Discuss the standards for each and how they are related to one another.

4. Consider what problems are not solved when a staff is used up.

5. Describe your team's solution thinking and acting, noting recent examples of successes.

6. Describe examples of substandard customer service or inadequate problem solving. Ask the team why these occurred.

7. Design a plan that is unique to your team, using the 12 action steps from the book. Openly evaluate success or failure of each step.

Questions:

1. What are your team's incidents and issues that must be addressed?

2. What parts of these incidents and issues can be traced directly to leadership dysfunction or lack of growing relationships?

3. How did you answer the questions in Lesson 34?

4. What behavioral changes will you make to enhance your leadership and your team's effectiveness?

5. What relational and functional strengths or weakness are revealed in your group's words and deeds?

Application:

Lessons I am learning:

Truths I will teach:

Actions I will take:

Results I will expect:

Lesson 35
Goals

Comments:

1. Identify your core team's strengths and weaknesses in goal fulfillment.

2. Develop grids of measurement of success or failure for your group's current endeavors.

3. Describe the team's strengths and weaknesses in their collective and individual utilization of time, target, and treasure.

4. Ask the team to explain goal fulfillment in light of their Code of Achievement (see page 43).

5. Comparisons of this kind compose healthy elements of relational and functional evaluation.

6. Transferring ownership of a goal means that the ones tasked with fulfillment possess the processes of action and closure with the leader's encouragement, investment, support, and coaching.

7. Transferring ownership requires the people tasked with goal fulfillment to report progress to those who need to know this information.

Questions:

1. Why is a goal not taken seriously?

2. Why is a goal a positive motivator?

3. What necessary tools are required to complete your next project and who will supply them?

4. Who should prioritize the action steps that are required to fulfill a goal?

5. What are indicators that transfer of ownership is not working?

6. What are indicators that transfer of ownership is working extremely well?

7. What kinds of celebrations should accompany goal fulfillments and when should they occur?

Application:

Lessons I am learning:

Truths I will teach:

Actions I will take:

Results I will expect:

Lesson 36
Restoring Relationships on a Team

Comments:

1. Among the signs of broken relationships are these:
   a. Isolationism
   b. Avoidance
   c. Gossip
   d. Refusing responsibility
   e. Fault finding
   f. Criticism
   g. Attacks
   h. Grudges
   i. Hostility
   j. Putdowns
   k. Defense postures
   l. Argumentative attitudes
   m. Negative and destructive conversations
   n. Absence
   o. Refusals to engage in open dialogue about solutions
   p. Anger

2. When these negative behaviors are revealed they should not be avoided, tolerated, or continually excused.

3. When a strong leader discovers incidents of behavioral dysfunction, that leader moves quickly to identify issues.

4. When issues are identified, parties who want solutions can be brought together to restore relationships.

5. Agreement on issues can lead to discussions based on values, paving the way for improved behaviors.

6. Of the seven leader responsibilities, name the ones that are the most difficult to accomplish.

7. When the next opportunity for restoring relationships comes, track your progress on the basis of the seven steps.

Questions:

1. In a broken relationship what behaviors are too often tolerated, where a team or leader simply hopes the dysfunction will simply go away?

2. What are the challenges, if any, of beginning a restoration meeting with the question, "Upon what do you agree?"

3. What values do negative behaviors violate?

4. What role does forgiveness play in restoring relationships and who should bring this up?

5. When should a leader not try to restore relationships on a team?

Application:

Lessons I am learning:

Truths I will teach:

Actions I will take:

Results I will expect:

Lesson 37

Emerging Leadership, Building People—It's Not New

Comments:

1. Describe the challenges and opportunities for a leader who demonstrates preferred behaviors *to* the follower before requiring them *from* the follower.

2. Define behaviors that openly demonstrate that people are more valuable than production.

3. When a leader promotes a follower's win, the leader does not own the follower's success; rather, the leader provides assistance, tools, coaching, and encouragement.

4. Leaders who invest in followers demonstrate willingness to risk for the follower's benefits. Name the risks you as a leader are willing to take, such as allocating time, energy, and other resources. Describe how you would use these resources to help a follower succeed and the results you would expect from this investment.

Questions:

1. Effective leadership is based on building relationships. If this concept is new to your core team's members, when did they first hear about it?

2. What about this "new" leadership is considered "soft?"

3. Because important, life changing decisions are only seen in altered behaviors, what behavioral changes should a leader and team expect to make when they willfully decide to place people over production and build relationships over function?

4. What positive and enduring legacies could be created from a team who divests shallow and tired ways of interaction and invests in time-tested and verified ways of working together?

Application:

Lessons I am learning:

Truths I will teach:

Actions I will take:

Results I will expect:

Lesson 38
It's All About Details

Comments:

1. Ask your team to name the small O-ring details of your operation and their importance.

2. Chart your answers to the questions posed in Lesson 38. Discuss those to which names have not yet been attached. Assign the names, calendar the actions, and identify the reporting systems.

3. Describe an unhealthy or unaccountable working atmosphere. List the details that often go unnoticed, are late in achievement, or remain undone when this dysfunction is allowed to continue.

4. The domino effects of attention, or lack of attention, to detail can be monumental. Describe the positive results when details are handled well and the negative consequences when they are not.

5. Great leaders and teams do not embrace "holding each other accountable." They learn, educate, and act upon each person holding him or herself accountable. Personal strength and endurance produce cooperative accountability.

6. Where individual accountability is present, a detail-oriented staff does not engage in micromanaging.

7. A leader shows followers how to handle important details through the leader's example and instruction.

8. Personality is not a cause of success or failure in handling details. Dealing with important small items is a choice.

9. A detail-oriented staff never assumes that consistency of action will occur, even though they may count on it. Instead, they teach, encourage, provide, report, and celebrate it.

Questions:

1. What aspects of your operation lag in the details?

2. Who owns chasing down information and reporting?

3. If team members think that holding each other accountable is a solution, how can a leader change this misperception to show that ownership of accountability is an individual's responsibility?

4. What are the details that are always done, those your team consistently relies upon, and who is accountable for their fulfillment?

5. What are ways that personality is used as an excuse for not handling the small but significant tasks?

6. When the team handles details well, how does it represent its product and its people?

Application:

Lessons I am learning:

Truths I will teach:

Actions I will take:

Results I will expect:

Lesson 39
Leaders Communicate

Comments:

1. Leaders initiate effective communication. Recall examples of proactive and desirable communication instigated by your leader.

2. Communication is not complete until behaviors change.

3. Clarity in communication may be better achieved when dialogue replaces monologue.

4. Evaluate communication in your work place. Determine how much is dialogue vs. monologue, which is preferred, and in what circumstances either one is best.

5. Because listening is a vital part of communication, name methods of effective listening that demonstrate receptivity. Describe which of these methods you and your team employ and which you should start to use.

Questions:

1. What are the greatest challenges to listening well?

2. How should barriers to listening be removed?

3. What are the signs and signals of failed communication?

4. What are methods your team uses to assure that what is said is what is heard and vice versa?

5. How often are effective methods of communication not taught, rather assumed?

6. How often should instruction occur on preferred methods of communication?

7. What are examples of excellent communication on your team?

Application:

Lessons I am learning:

Truths I will teach:

Actions I will take:

Results I will expect:

Lesson 40
It's About Time

Comments:

1. Name the benefits of placing assignments and actions on calendars, and making this information available to the people who should have access to it.

2. Discuss why publishing calendars can meet with resistance.

3. People who want to use time well hold themselves accountable.

4. Describe the differences between treating time as a treasure and treating it as a burden.

5. "Make the most of your time" is good advice.

6. Time management is all about exercising discipline and taking responsibility.

7. Wasting time is a mark of struggling character.

Questions:

1. What are the domino effects when time is not utilized well by members of the core team?

2. What are the results of chronic lateness?

3. What does one person's lateness say about how much he or she values other people and their time?

4. What are examples of strong accountability on a team whose members treat time as a precious resource?

5. How does your team handle due dates?

Application:

Lessons I am learning:

Truths I will teach:

Actions I will take:

Results I will expect:

Lesson 41
Planning

Comments:

1. Describe a successful plan that your team composed and completed.

2. Discuss the importance of timelines in the creation and implementation of a plan.

3. Reporting systems and communication pathways should never be assumed, but articulated decisively and referenced often.

4. Plans that become accountable actions produce measurable results.

5. The larger the responsibilities may be, the more that planning should accompany their design and implementation.

6. Successful planning eventually boils down to performing specific actions— some large, some small—all of which are vital to the accomplishment of the plan.

7. Describe why large and small roles should be assigned as part of planning and execution.

Questions:

1. Why do innovative people sometimes balk at planning?

2. Why do dedicated planners sometimes resist innovation?

3. What roles do creative thinking and taking risks play when a team designs a plan?

4. What part does personal accountability have in the execution of a plan and how should the team be informed that its members are fulfilling individual roles and responsibilities?

5. As a plan unfolds, what measurements of success or failure should be utilized?

6. How are planning and setting goals connected?

7. What are the inhibitors of effective planning and how does your team address them?

Application:

Lessons I am learning:

Truths I will teach:

Actions I will take:

Results I will expect:

Lesson 42
Profit Centers

Comments:

1. Discuss what the term *profit margin* means to your core team.

2. List the means your team uses to determine what is profitable and what isn't.

3. Identify the circumstances, forces, or controls that inhibit profit from being realized in both people and production.

4. Describe business situations where profit is not the goal.

5. Relate desires to increase profit margins to this phrase: "The ends will not justify our means if the processes include sacrificing our character."

Questions:

1. How does your team know it is profitable?

2. What are your team's tangible profits?

3. What are your team's intangible profits?

4. How are tangible and intangible profits related to planning, time management, production, and accountability?

5. How do your organization's customers know they are more important than what they purchase?

Application:

Lessons I am learning:

Truths I will teach:

Actions I will take:

Results I will expect:

Lesson 43

Principles in Practice—Where Rubber Meets Road

Comments:

1. Describe the connections between principles and practices, words and works.

2. Relate examples from recent activities on your team that illustrate these connecting points.

3. Leaders form a model and set the pace for exemplary behaviors.

4. Aligning principles and practices requires leaders and followers to model what they want from each other.

Questions:

1. Which of the team's core principles are more difficult to practice and why?

2. What examples from leadership that demonstrate stronger alignment of principles and practices would your core team like to see?

3. What is a follower's responsibility when a leader is not practicing principles in the workplace?

4. What are some of the major challenges that accompany a personal decision to alter behavior to cooperate with principle?

Application:

Lessons I am learning:

Truths I will teach:

Actions I will take:

Results I will expect:

Lesson 44

Without Decisive Action, It's Worthless

Comments:

1. Compose a list of agenda items from your team meetings that have fallen into the "We need…" category of discussion without action.

2. Creative ideas are valuable but remain as concepts until plans and actions accompany them.

3. List the expectations of delivery that must be present once a decision is made on a proposed idea.

4. Describe reporting systems and timelines your team employs when they turn discussions into deeds.

Questions:

1. What are the difficulties inherent in turning deliberations into actions?

2. How valuable is calendaring action to solve problems?

3. Why is preparation important before someone says, "We need…?"

4. When could not saying "We need..." constitute avoidance of a problem that requires resolution?

Application:

Lessons I am learning:

Truths I will teach:

Actions I will take:

Results I will expect:

Lesson 45
Absentee Leadership

Comments:

1. Hidden agendas often accompany absentee leadership, regardless of its form.

2. Absenteeism, at its root, is avoidance of connection.

3. Describe the results when a leader chooses to be absent.

4. Describe the expectations of improved core team behaviors when a leader is present.

5. Engaged leaders want their followers to know where they are and how they manage their work time.

6. A calendar of work activity should be published for those who need to know.

7. Accountability is demonstrated when the administrative support team knows how to answer the question of where the boss is.

8. A team is not healthy when members feel they must hold each other accountable.

Questions:

1. Of the four examples of absentee leadership—physical, emotional, mental, or figurative—which does your team think does the most damage to the team's health and well being?

2. What should a leader's response be to a follower who exercises absenteeism?

3. What is a follower's responsibility, if any, to confront a leader who is absent?

4. What are the benefits to a team when a leader is not absent, rather fully present and accounted for?

5. What kinds of communication prove a leader is present and fully engaged?

Application:

Lessons I am learning:

Truths I will teach:

Actions I will take:

Results I will expect:

Lesson 46
When Followers Take Initiative

Comments:

1. Initiative is taken seriously when creative ideas originate from faithful people.

2. A secure leader, especially one that wants success for his or her followers, will welcome initiative from core team members.

3. An insecure leader may discourage innovative thinking.

4. Whenever a team member, regardless of position, takes the initiative, that person is leading.

Questions:

1. When a leader is threatened by a follower's initiative, how should the team deal with it?

2. When a follower refuses to take initiative what should the leader do?

3. What motivates you to take initiative?

4. How should a leader encourage followers to take initiative?

Application:

Lessons I am learning:

Truths I will teach:

Actions I will take:

Results I will expect:

Lesson 47
Leading From the Middle

Comments:

1. List the fears that prevent a team member from exercising leadership from the middle, or from below the top.

2. Identify the positive values that are violated when these fears exist.

3. Violations of values contribute to destroying relationships, inhibiting innovative thinking, and stifling solution provision.

4. Come up with a list of changes you believe your organization or team needs to make.

5. Determine which of your behaviors earn you the right to be heard in expressing your ideas for change.

6. Since leadership is seen when people take initiative, then the inhibitors to considering innovative changes may be the ineffective behaviors of those with the ideas for change.

7. Changing a workplace is all about altering personal behaviors, first.

Questions:

1. Why should a leader be concerned about a follower who continually comes up with ideas for change but doesn't demonstrate a solid work ethic? What should the leader do about it?

2. What should a faithful follower expect from a leader when he or she presents ideas for necessary change?

3. If a leader is intimidated by a strong follower who wants positive change, that leader may be insecure. How should the leader and core team address this issue?

4. When excuses for not leading from below the top are offered, what values are violated?

5. What disciplines should a committed and accountable follower exercise in approaching the subject of change with a great leader?

Application:

Lessons I am learning:

Truths I will teach:

Actions I will take:

Results I will expect:

Lesson 48
Problem Solving Techniques

Comments:

1. Describe which of the first four action stages of problem solving—common ground, common good, common goal, common gains—are the most difficult to engage and why.

2. Discuss problem solving techniques your team has tried that have failed to produce successful outcomes.

3. Place a current problem into the action stages. Determine its status. Consider what actions must occur to move the process toward solution design and fulfillment.

4. A great leader teaches problem solving principles and practices to his or her followers.

5. Uncommon results become common outcomes for a team that faithfully applies the action stages of problem resolution and takes them to term.

Questions:

1. What characterizes an environment of ownership of responsibility?

2. What characteristics of weak leadership are demonstrated when unresolved issues are continually tolerated or excused?

3. How does your team define a solution provision mind-set?

4. What are the inhibitors to creating atmospheres of solution thinking and acting?

5. How would shared responsibility, accountability, and faithfulness cooperate in solving a problem your team currently faces?

Application:

Lessons I am learning:

Truths I will teach:

Actions I will take:

Results I will expect:

Lesson 49
How Leaders Handle Discouragement

Comments:

1. Discouragement and encouragement are strong forces. Neither should be denied nor refused.

2. Discouragement is reaction and encouragement is pro-action.

3. Leaders who are discouraged may not be weak, but they may be tired and tried.

4. Great leaders who handle discouragement well focus on higher motives and superior means to help solve immediate and future problems.

5. Explain how the law of sowing and reaping and the law of compensation help to put discouragement in its rightful place.

Questions:

1. How do you face discouragement?

2. When sources of discouragement are uncovered, how should they be evaluated as to short term or long term importance?

3. When a leader works through discouragement, what kinds of clarity should be expected and what actions should result?

4. In what forums and forms should a great leader discuss discouragement with his or her team?

5. What examples of handling discouragement can you remember that encouraged you?

Application:

Lessons I am learning:

Truths I will teach:

Actions I will take:

Results I will expect:

Lesson 50

Winning or Whining—What Do You Encourage?

Comments:

1. List specific actions that showcase winning attitudes.

2. List specific actions that whiners demonstrate.

3. Describe the benefits and detriments of each list.

4. Attitude is a choice.

5. The choice of an attitude is evidenced in words and works.

Questions:

1. When winning attitudes are present, what are the results?

2. How should a leader deal with whiners on a team?

3. Of the four solution-thinking decisions that accompany winners, which of these is the whiner likely to not comprehend or decide is not worth the effort?

4. Why does confronting problems with positive planning and action steps work?

Application:

Lessons I am learning:

Truths I will teach:

Actions I will take:

Results I will expect:

Lesson 51

Opportunities for Leadership Come From Circumstances and They Are Created

Comments:

1. Name opportunities your leader created in which you grew in understanding and action.

2. Recall circumstances where your leadership rose to new heights of effectiveness.

3. Part of preparation is rehearsing for the bad times.

4. Describe your team's readiness to confront challenges and rise above them.

5. A leader who wants his or her team to be prepared may consider various actions to help the team get ready. Name some of these actions you and your team feel would be beneficial.

6. Elements of preparation include seeing the big picture, offering instruction, providing necessary tools, and understanding individual roles.

7. Great leaders help followers learn and grow when circumstances change, and when the circumstances need to be changed.

Questions:

1. When can a leader overdo preparation?

2. How can a leader help a team not to be overwhelmed in the midst of negative circumstances?

3. How should a leader help a team member who is not responding well to adverse occurrences?

4. What are reasonable risks that could enhance learning?

5. What kinds of resistance should a team and its leader expect in difficult times, regardless of sources?

Application:

Lessons I am learning:

Truths I will teach:

Actions I will take:

Results I will expect:

Lesson 52

You Are More Important Than What You Do

Comments:

1. Ask the core team to evaluate how they believe their leader views him or herself.

2. Affirm your leader relationally and functionally. Be event and time specific.

3. The character of a leader is seen in how the leader respects his or her person.

4. A leader cannot share strong relationships unless and until that leader possesses healthy dignity and pride.

5. The leader's model of relational and functional balance will be revealed in the attitudes and actions of the team.

Questions:

1. What stands in the way of people becoming convinced that they are more important than what they do?

2. If you were convinced you were more important than what you do, who would benefit?

3. What are the differences between healthy and unhealthy pride?

4. What is your definition of dignity and self worth?

5. What personal applications of the Code of Achievement are revealed in your leadership?

6. What improvements in your leadership would come from deciding how important you are?

7. How do humility and the recognition of worth cooperate in a balanced individual?

Application:

Lessons I am learning:

Truths I will teach:

Actions I will take:

Results I will expect:

Closing

Reminders and resources are requisites in human experience. Commitments toward reaching positive life change are reinforced when endearing and enduring principles and practices are repeatedly brought to the forefront of thinking and acting.

Values compose a core team's skeleton truths, the foundations on which a healthy organization is built. A core team's vision, mission, and message rest upon its values. Upon these, their Code of Achievement, great teams contribute reliable words and responsible works.

L.E.A.D.—Learning, Education, Action, Destiny and *Leadership Works* comprise a collection of leadership truths to read, a teaching tool to sow productive seed, and a reference manual to revisit in thought and deed. Use the book and study guide to empower your teams as you reinforce concepts and practices within yourself.

Learn, educate, and act upon one lesson every week of the year. This may be one method of involvement and investment that produces strengthened relationships and superior functions.

Live what you learn and teach. Your team's destiny will develop and legacy will form as you climb the mountain of principled leadership.
1. *Adapt* the lessons to your environment and teach them in your own words.
2. *Adopt* learned and life-altering behaviors into your experiences. Teach your team through words and examples. Create duplicative models as you engage with your followers.

Learn, educate, and act. Form a destiny that leaves a positive legacy of impact, influence, and investment. Processing new information and turning it into viable and verifiable living is a golden opportunity for people who want to grow. It is a worthy option for any leader who desires enduring results.

You are encouraged to heed what you read. You are empowered to grow and to L.E.A.D.

When will you begin? By what criteria will you measure gains, correct errors, and celebrate successes in yourself and your teams?

Creative
Team
Resources
Group

www.ctrg.com
www.LeadershipIs.com
www.IndustrialStrengthSolutions.com
www.CoreTeamsWork.com
www.Lead52.com
www.Lincoln-Leadership-Gettysburg.com

CTRG provides quality resources for the development of teams within organizations whose desires are to grow and develop their personnel and achieve greater results in product or service provision. CTRG gives people great information that allows them to make changes in how they live and work and does this through building core teams. Our resources include personnel training, seminars, counsel, one-on-one and small-group leadership coaching, books, and instruction manuals.

Our foundational principle is that people are more important than production and relationships precede and give definition to function. The value of a person's contributions comes from that person's inherent worth. The value of the person causes the contributions a person makes to achieve even greater results.

Contact CTRG at the websites above. We will demonstrate first-hand how our team building principles can work for you. Glen Aubrey, President and CEO, along with other CTRG staff are available to your group for speaking engagements, on-site training and leadership coaching. CTRG looks forward to serving and working with you!

The Author

Glen Aubrey is President and CEO of Creative Team Resources Group, Inc. (CTRG), www.ctrg.com. He is an author, business consultant, leadership trainer, conference speaker, professional musician, music writer and orchestrator, and poet. He has authored *Leadership Is—How to Build Your Legacy, Industrial Strength Solutions Build Successful Work Teams!, Core Teams Work Their Principles and Practices, Growing Core Teams, Core Team Impact!, Go From the Night, Arranging Notes, L.E.A.D.— Learning, Education, Action, Destiny,* and *Lincoln, Leadership and Gettysburg.*

You are invited to visit these websites:
www.ctrg.com
www.CreativeTeamPublishing.com
www.LeadershipIs.com
www.IndustrialStrengthSolutions.com
www.CoreTeamsWork.com
www.Lincoln-Leadership-Gettysburg.com
www.GoFromTheNight.com
www.Lead52.com
www.glenaubrey.com

The Publisher

Creative Team Publishing (CTP) is a division of Creative Team Resources Group, Inc. (CTRG, www.ctrg.com). CTP was formed in 2007 to publish and distribute business and team development, leadership training, and poetry books, as well as literature of inspiration, insight, human achievement, and positive general interest.

The company's commitment is to make high quality literature available and engage in excellence throughout the process of publication. Customer satisfaction is a top priority. Because CTP practices due diligence in selecting which books it will publish, CTP chooses to work with customers who meet a qualified standard of literary competence and uplifting content.

CTP is a fee-for-service publisher. Products offered include the following:

Pre-Press
1. Editing
2. Proofing
3. Revision
4. Typesetting
5. Four Color Cover Design
6. ISBN
7. Print Set-up

Post-Press
1. Product supply
2. Press releases

Contact Creative Team Publishing. Please visit our company website, www.CreativeTeamPublishing.com, for information. We look forward to reviewing your literary creation.

Products

Books and Curriculum by Glen Aubrey
Available through Creative Team Resources Group, Inc.
Online Store
www.ctrg.com

Leadership Is— How to Build Your Legacy

Industrial Strength Solutions Build Successful Work Teams!

Core Teams Work Their Principles and Practices

Lincoln, Leadership and Gettysburg

Go From the Night

L.E.A.D.—Learning, Education, Action, Destiny

Leadership Works—Advanced Study Guide for L.E.A.D.

Growing Core Teams

Core Team Impact!

Arranging Notes

Music CD Recordings by Glen Aubrey
Available through Creative Team Resources Group, Inc.
Online Store
www.ctrg.com

Beautiful, A Symphonic Experience
Music by Lindamarie Todd and Glen Aubrey

Born Is the King
Christmas Keyboard Reflections
Piano solos

The Custom Album
Piano Solos by Glen Aubrey

Go From the Night Meditation
Glen Aubrey, Solo Piano
Pat Kelley, Guitars
Go From the Night Selected Readings

Meditation
Glen Aubrey, Solo Piano
Pat Kelley, Guitars

Reflecting Hymn
The Rock Album
Piano solos

Timeless
Piano Solos
Original Songs by Glen Aubrey

What Child Is This
Glen Aubrey, Solo Piano

www.ingramcontent.com/pod-product-compliance
Lightning Source LLC
Chambersburg PA
CBHW081106220326
41598CB00038B/7255